Me Poems:

A Passionate Glimpse Of Life Through Poetry The Early Years: Book One

Written By Ing Ledlie

Illustrated by Ing and Zarah Ledlie

Copyright © 2023 by Ing Ledlie. All rights reserved.

No part of this book may be reproduced or used in any manner without written permission of the copyright owner, except for the use of quotations in a book review.
For more information, email: ingledlie@gmail.com

First paperback edition 2023.

Published by Me and Mister C Publishing;
Goulburn, NSW Australia.

A catalogue for this work is available from the National Library of Australia.

ISBN 978-0-6457553-0-5

www.meandmisterc.com

Illustrations copyright © 2023 by Ing and Zarah Ledlie.

Medium used for illustrations: Graphite pencil/ black ink.

Cover and book interior design by Fenton Creative.

For Cara; sisters share a special bond...

Nobody has ever measured, not even poets, how much a heart can hold.

Zelda Fitzgerald (1900–1948)
American writer

Contents

Foreword 1

Introduction 3

Acknowledgements 5

Flying Pigeon 7

The Surprise 8

Candy Girl 9

Candy Cat-Dam 11

Number Five 13

Seasons 15

Too Young 17

Rag Girl 19

Fire 21

Ray Of Sunshine 22

Lady Diana 23

The Wait 25

Home 26

Orange-Stained Clouds 27

Mrs Kent	28
The Verdant Light	29
Sacrifice	30
College Life	31
Plea	32
The Door	33
Innocence	34
The War Game	35
Ponder of Love	36
The Mosquito	37
Exclusive	38
Love Sphere	39
Handsome	40
The Wombat's Dilemma	41
Face of Innocence	42
Gateway	43

Foreword

I am honoured to write the foreword of the book, Me Poems: A Glimpse Of Life Through Poetry The Early Years, written by Ing Ledlie and also Illustrated by Ing and her younger daughter Zarah. Having worked in the field of nursing for nearly fifteen years, the last ten plus I have had the privilege of working in the mental health field. I am an advocate for positive expression of mental health in the community, and encourage healthy ways of coping, while working with and supporting people. I can appreciate the need to develop safe ways in expressing and managing one's life's traumas and triumphs.

I have known Ing Ledlie for the better part of twenty-three years. We met through mutual friends and instantly developed our unique friendship. I always remember Ing Ledlie as a kindred spirit, someone who is passionate and busily creating. We share many passions in life, including our love of nursing, self-reflection and health promotion. Now in our third decade of friendship, we continue to support each other through life with our experiences of life, love and loss.

When I read this book, I felt transported. I treasured reading all thirty poems in their most natural and beautiful form. Every emotion including, joy, excitement, shame, guilt and fear has developed through this journey in life. Ing Ledlie has bravely crafted and shared her writing to make sense of the world, as a way of coping with recent and previous trauma.

The connection to imaginary friends, safe places and helping to hide from fear, loss and shame as depicted through both the poetry and illustrations, are enlightening. Overcoming the sometimes-challenging experiences and emotions faced through life's journey, and by giving these emotions a voice, becomes a powerful tool for all to combat in life.

I hope this book will provide encouragement for you, the reader, to start your own journey in expressing your own emotions in life, as a way of finding your own voice and healthy medium.

Donna Preston-Bond
Mental Health Registered Nurse

My best friend is the one who brings out the best in me.

Henry Ford (1863–1947)
American Industrialist

Introduction

We all know life can be tough to navigate, particularly in our current climate and times. Passion is what makes us who we are; expressing feelings openly and safely is beneficial to our healthy minds and bodies. This is certainly the case with poetry and me, and is central to this compilation. Writing has always been my passion. Starting from an early age, I began expressing my emotions through the written word as a way to escape from difficult and traumatic experiences. And while at times also joyous and memorable ones.

Whether you, the reader, be a young adult or a mature reader, this book is an emotive compilation aimed towards every generation and has been developed to provoke passion and inclusion. My hope is that this compilation is thought-provoking and allows you, to explore your own emotions and also to experience self-reflection and an awareness of life, love, loss, healing, and well-being.

Following a serious car accident towards the latter part of 2022, my life and my family's lives changed dramatically. I was faced with numerous challenging emotions throughout my slow recovery. I found myself lost in self-pity, and at times engulfed in anger, frustration, sadness, and hopelessness through my ever-changing situation. I finally found solace in my writing after having major neck surgery, resulting from injuries I sustained in the accident.

I was grateful to begin sitting at my laptop again, having the time to write poetry due to not being able to return to nursing. My world settled as I started to write, even while I was in the hospital. This greatly enabled me to move forward on my journey to recovery, as it also reduced my feelings of stress and anxiety. Through these unexpected experiences, I can deeply express a greater understanding of how precious and short life really is.

During these months, I had an overwhelming desire to read, edit, and self-publish my life's poetry. I feel it is now time to share, so, without further ado, I give you book one: Me Poems: The Early Years, a passionate glimpse of my life through poetry.

Ing Ledlie
Author

Where there is love there is life.

Indira Gandhi (1917–1984)
Indian Prime Minister

Acknowledgements

I would like to firstly thank you, the reader, for taking the time to view this book of poetry. The unexpected opportunity to create and share this book, has brought an immense amount of satisfaction to me as a writer. I am honoured to have had the opportunity to collaborate and create the illustrations depicted in this book with my younger daughter, Zarah. Words cannot fully convey my love and gratitude to my husband, children, family, and friends for their unwavering care and support. A heartfelt thanks also goes out to my editor and designer. Without your longstanding support, I would not be able to do what I do, so thank-you!

> *The past was.*
> *Tomorrow may be.*
> *Only today is.*
>
> Beth Mende Conny (1955–)
> American born writer

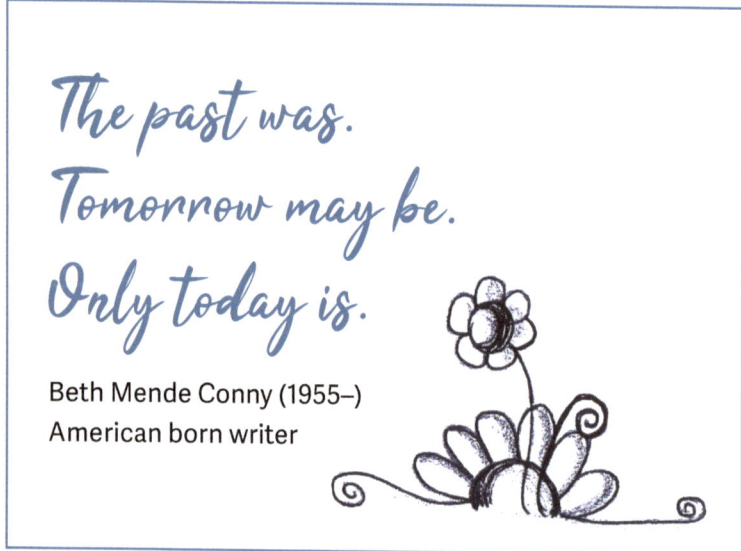

There are two ways to live: you can live as if nothing is a miracle; you can live as if everything is a miracle.

Albert Einstein (1879–1955)
German-born American physicist

Flying Pigeon

November 1983

I saw a pigeon in my backyard trying to fly,
it flapped its wings, it tried to go up high.

The pigeon had a tiny head and a big tummy,
I think it ate too much; it was rather hungry.

The grey and tan pigeon tried to take off,
its wings wouldn't work, a dud blast-off?

Finally, the pigeon's wings took up speed,
its little legs got moving, there was a need.

The little pigeon chirped with much delight,
it did finally take its first long magical flight.

The pigeon flew high, it disappeared out of sight,
I thought I'd lost it forever; it did give me a fright!

The pigeon flew three times around the world,
it was gone for many days, or so I later heard.

The pigeon flew back in our yard, like a super-fast meteor,
it pooped on my head! Gee, that hasn't happened before...

The Surprise

February 1984

There was a wriggling lump in my bed,
pulling back the doona, I saw part of you.

First, I saw your white striped curling tail,
then I saw your patterned soft-looking fur.

I heard a quiet noise and then another.
Did I just hear that? It was a soft meow.

Could that really and truly be you?
A very cute you, hiding in my bed!

I pulled back more of the floral sheet,
a white paw snuck out to tap my hand.

I climbed onto my bed to get closer,
to see who was purring in my bed.

I took a breath and opened my eyes,
you were my real, soft birthday gift.

I named you Candy because you were
all covered in stripes, just like a lollipop!

You had a pink bow around your neck,
and, of course, you were so very sweet.

Such a cute green-eyed striped present,
you were my new special cuddly kitten.

Candy Girl

August 1985

Candy girl was my sweet striped cat,
who loved sleeping under our beds.
Candy girl was my furry best friend.
Together, we'd play outside for hours.

Candy climbed up trees in our backyard,
I followed, chasing her up so very high.
I'd get in trouble, my mother would shout,
to get down and not wear my white jeans.

I couldn't help it; I loved being up high,
amongst the glorious trees to smell the air.
I'd spy other curious creatures and animals,
finding the cranky magpie's nest & worms.

Candy met another cat, a big male cat,
we named him Tom, short for Tomcat.
Tom had a deep meow; he was persistent,
Tom stayed in our yard, playing with Candy.

Candy grew a belly, she then slept a lot,
she didn't climb trees nor play with me.
Our mother said she was becoming a dam,
I didn't understand that soon there'd be babies.

School finished; it was now the weekend,
Candy was acting strange and couldn't walk.
Candy loved laying on our velvet beanbag.
Patting Candy, I gave her a bowl of milk.

The next morning, there was much commotion,
looking in the rumpus room, I saw a big mess.
Candy was exhausted but looked up purring.
She had given birth to eight furry baby-kittens!

We quietly watched Candy clean her cat babies,
we weren't able to hold them for some time yet.
Candy became a caring new cat dam-mother,
but she didn't play with me much after that.

Candy Cat-Dam

November 1985

The kittens were fun. Choosing their names,
my sister and I knew it was a lot of work.
Each kitten had different cute personalities,
I grew fond of the small one named Runtie.

Big Tom came into our yard a few times,
you couldn't miss his profound loud call.
Hissing, he saw the kittens through the door,
Candy was busy: she didn't play with Tom.

Days later, persistent Tom got in the house
while my sister and I were still at school.
Not working, my mother said she was out,
we came home to sadness and quite a fright.

Tom attacked Candy and her small kittens,
my mother upset; our stepfather grew angry.
We lost three of our sweet babies that day,
Candy and her babies were taken to the vet.

My mother found homes for the kittens,
I asked to keep one, our cute little Runtie.
My mother refused, no explanation why,
I grew resentful: she showed little care.

I helped Candy. She liked licking my fingers,
she wasn't the same. Something was wrong.
She didn't climb trees or run very much,
her fur became matted. She then grew thin.

Home from school, and no Candy under my bed,
searching everywhere, I called out her name.
Our mother called us, Candy had been sick
at the vet, Candy then went to pet heaven.

Sadness fenced me in. I felt quite numb,
anger grew inside of me, no-one listened.
I wasn't allowed to keep our Runtie kitten,
I didn't say goodbye to my Candy cat-dam.

Number Five

January 1986

Number five was our home, my mother,
stepfather, my sister and I lived for a time.
Our stepfather's four children often stayed,
a glimpse of happiness sometimes showed.

School-holiday fun days came and went,
my sister and I loved our big trampoline.
The soft black mat underneath our heads,
our bodies and legs were warm and cosy.

Running to the side of our house, we'd
pull the long green hose and turn it on.
Jumping as the sprinkler sprayed cool
droplets of water under the trampoline.

Time forgotten, my sister and I played,
giggling while chasing each other around.
Jumping off, we ran under the cherry tree,
giving us shade in the middle of our garden.

We'd splash water and catch our breath,
then climb the makeshift wooden ladder.
Up to our cool, private cubby house
that our stepfather had carefully built.

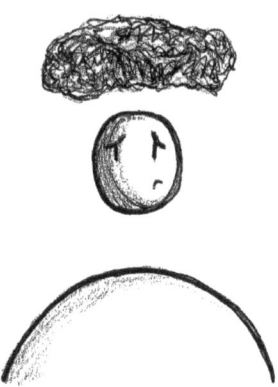

Wafts of freshly homemade pies and jams,
came out of our nearby kitchen window.
A whiff catching our small freckled noses,
an indication it was soon time for lunch.

My sister and I would soon climb down,
the most glorious cherry tree ever seen.
Chatting about our fun plans to extend
the slippery mud hole we had created.

Our mother was distracted, baking again,
it seemed like she was in there for hours.
Some afternoons we'd get a silver coin,
then be allowed to skip to the Candy Bar.

Staying away, we'd sit on the front porch,
dipping our lolly sticks in the pink sherbet.
Pulling me closer, my sister comforted me,
as we blocked out our parents' raised voices.

Seasons

August 1986

Number six was our rented home.
A peaceful place where trees stood tall.
Beds of every plant imaginable
bloomed in our makeshift garden space.
Our mother spent every possible hour
conversing plant encouragement.

Summer meant sweltering sleepless nights
and carefree weekends at the park
where my sister and I would run.
A good chance to play on the swings
I pretended I was a flying acrobat
performing in front of imaginary friends.

Soon Autumn arrived, as it snatched
all kinds of leaves from their places.
Such colourful debris to fall
cool might be the earth below
to roll around before the chores
was what I enjoyed most.

Winter came creeping in
thick grey stormy clouds
danced, devouring greedy mouthfuls.
Darkness succumbed to the street
drawn curtains swayed
in the cool, unearthly wind.

Doors shut tightly, a first crack
of thunder crashing over the sky;
concealing our parent's loud shouting.
A sigh of relief as the storm passed
for the sky revealed a restored day
and the chance for a dip in the pool.

Too Young

January 1987

Buttoning up my white denim jeans,
I turned to flush the porcelain toilet.
I saw something new, something red,
I began to worry as if I had cut myself.

A wave of dread came over me.
Did I just get that horrible thing,
that's supposed to happen to girls
who are much older, not now to me!

I washed my hands, trying to forget about
what I had just seen, I couldn't believe it.
I kept thinking to myself it's not happening,
I was carefree; I was known as a 'tomboy'.

I liked climbing trees and getting dirty,
I didn't care about frizzy hair or freckles.
Sitting on the sofa, another idea then stuck,
what if this was it, and I leaked everywhere?

I quickly got up, going back into the toilet,
I unbuttoned my white jeans and checked.
There it was again. Instant fear took over me,
I didn't have anything to soak up this mess.

Folding sheets of toilet paper, I placed them
in my pants, I buttoned my jeans back up.
That'll work. It will get me through this
bad kind of nightmare I was now living.

Later that day, the toilet paper didn't work
I would have to tell; it would be my mother.
I didn't know what was happening to me,
I'm too young was my next feared thought.

It was the end of the long school holidays,
I hadn't even finished primary school yet.
Driving home, my mother noticed I was off,
feeling sad, I said nothing; I didn't want a fuss.

Travelling in the old white car, I had to tell,
with little courage, I found it hard to speak.
Thinking I may get into some kind of trouble,
taking a breath, I squeaked and then let out a cry.

My mother stared blankly and shook her head,
doubting what I had seen. I cried even more.
Sighing, she claimed we needed some supplies,
not knowing what that meant, I quietly nodded.

In the car driving home, my mother was quiet,
her head turned; a tear rolled down her cheek.
I would have welcomed a hug, as for my mother,
nothing more was said. I felt quite like a leper.

Later I heard my mother tell our stepfather,
then my sister, who was surprised but kind.
She's too young, all my mother's friends said;
hearing whispers, I felt I was being watched.

Feelings of sadness, my life did change a lot,
innocence lost for things I did not understand.
I didn't mind my body, except for my big feet,
I liked being me; why did I have to grow up?

Rag Girl

May 1987

It was the end of the school holidays,
time to go back to school, it felt odd.
We were friends; maybe it'll be okay,
I did think you would have my back.

At school, I wanted to confess,
about the thing that girls did get.
Using the bathroom more now,
it was best to tell it to you straight.

You were distracted, finding it funny.
I didn't understand. You told others.
Whispering to classmates was unkind,
befriending other students, you teased.

The taunts began, and then the giggling,
I shrugged it off; it was your turn soon.
Calling me '*pad-girl*' you told the boys,
they laughed then called me '*rag-girl*'.

Trying to make it to assembly on time,
I leaked on the back of my school dress.
I went to the bathroom and only cried,
the boys laughed and teased far more.

My mother said no to me staying home.
I had an idea to bring my school jumper
if I leaked, I could tie it around my waist,
if I didn't quite make it to the bathroom.

You didn't understand. I tried to explain,
cruel taunts, your true colours did show.
Tears on the playground, but others helped,
telling our teacher, who rang my mother.

I was told to play with other friends,
you were moved to the composite class.
Taunts continued on the playground,
hey *'rag-girl'*, *'pad-girl'*, *'rag-girl'*...

I pleaded for you to finally stop,
you weren't my friend after all.
Friends didn't tease each other,
they just believed in one another.

Fire

October 1987

Fire is sparkling as it shines
stabbing at the wood,
vicious little flames
dancing as they should.
A grey wolf soon appears
jumping through the flames,
as if it has appeared maimed.
Looking for its life-long pair,
it dances and soon disappears.
And all that I can possibly see
to care, is the black charred
remains of the crackling coals
in the faded fire that once was.

Ray Of Sunshine

July 1988

Whenever things go wrong
and the pain begins to show,
I can help you when you're down
and ride away your gloomy frown.

A single violet in the soft earth
will once soon begin to bloom,
from the warmth and care
that we three do all share.

Your happiness means a mile
to me, as does that half smile,
my love for you is from the heart,
something that will never dart.

Remember when things go wrong
I'll be there to share a song,
to bring back that bright spark
from out of the deep lonely dark.

Emptiness and fear will soon disappear
it's a good thing we have you quite near,
your broken heart will once more sing
a small ray of sunshine will then begin.

Lady Diana

March 1988

I excitedly ran home, to tell my mother and sister
I was really lucky to be going to see Lady Diana.
My mother didn't believe me, and my sister was envious
as to why she wasn't meeting Lady Diana like me.

My school teacher rang my mother; it was 1983,
I was chosen as a reward for doing well in year four.
My teacher, classmates and I from our primary school
walked across the road to the New Parliament House.

My mother made a pretty posy from our rose garden,
I was nervous, and I carried the rose posy so very carefully.
I wore my long hair neat, my school shoes were shiny,
I couldn't wait to meet our People's Princess, Diana.

My heart skipped a beat. I stood behind the grey barrier,
I held the posy tight in my hands, the sun shone brightly.
Not wanting to miss it, my teacher stood right next to me,
two men in suits led me through the side of the barrier.

I heard lots of cheering and then my squeals of delight,
I stood very still; in my mind, I practiced my best curtsy.
I then saw her looking like a beautiful glowing mirage,
I didn't believe my eyes; my hand shielded the hot sun.

Glowing in an elegant peach-coloured dress and hat,
it was our beautiful Diana, my star, our people's idol.
I tried to curtsy, then handed the Princess my posy,
never forgetting the way she looked at me and smiled.

My mother told all her friends I had met Lady Diana,
my teacher was proud of our happy classmates and me.
I made it in the local school paper, my mother then kept,
it was my one happy memory wading through year four.

The Wait

March 1989

She silently waits, contemplating,
wishing the loneliness to disappear.

A land of impossible never,
is where she has been wed.

Her inner self grows in strength,
as the harsh sun slowly fades down.

Her compassion becomes more wary,
as a child's lost voice is soon found.

Although the years grow shorter,
and the contentment is hers to see.

She silently waits and then waits,
for her cruel husband to soon leave.

To regain her life, her self-worth,
and for her mind to then be set free.

Home

June 1989

Cold creaking wooden floor
old musty sour urine smells.
Toes that could wriggle
through worn broken shoes.
A worn iron-cast bed,
a rotten stained mattress,
home.

A tall, thin pallid body
a faded pink calico dress.
Alone in the far corner
hidden by fearful shadows.
She is trapped by timidity
and held by her own tears,
home.

A mug of dirty water
stale buttered bread.
Holes in the drafty door
ceiling scarred with stains.
No laughter, no warmth
walls lived in poverty,
home.

Orange-Stained Clouds

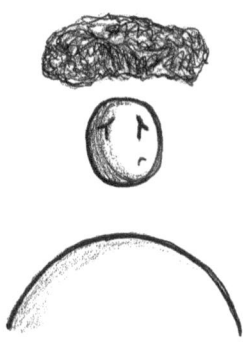

October 1990

Gasping while quietly whimpering
she struggled to keep her balance.
But again, it came and again
like fingers dipped into hot fire,
digging into her tender flesh.

Her thin naked body trembled
but she held her head up high.
Blood trickled down her pale legs,
staining the calico smock that hung
in shreds around her tiny ankles.

Oh, how that cracking sound of leather
on her skin killed every breath of sound.
Her weak body no longer responded
her mind no longer answered
because again and again, it came.

Her threshold now well passed
her faltering knees collapsed.
Her last recollection that day
was of the orange-stained clouds
that streaked the pale grey sky.

Mrs Kent

November 1990

Next door she did live
intriguing was her back garden
where no lawn could possibly grow.
It housed many giant fruit trees
delicious to pocket the figs, pears
and the juicy dark blood plums,
her name was Mrs Kent.

A home-bound manner
floral frocks and knitted cardigans
with glistening oval buttons.
Netted, silver-peppered hair
clear, hazel eyes that shone
seeing the world as a curious place,
her name was Mrs Kent.

Soft wrinkles and a distinct laugh,
our moving day soon arrived
no more skipping next door
to munch on juicy blood plums
and drink flat, sweetened lemonade.
Years later I heard she had passed,
her name was Mrs Kent.

The Verdant Light

May 1991

She's waiting for the verdant light
her floral dress jerks over her body.
Her clumsy heavy feet cannot hold
the swift sway she cannot keep still.

Carefully she has been dressed,
I'm here, I'm here, look at me!
Her constant wriggling struggles
grasp me like a silent whisper.

When I see her face, it is freckled
to remind me of cousins, of myself.
How rigid her limbs do remind me
of how straight my own spine is.

And when the lights do finally change
she skips then dances across the road.
Leaving us all behind like a shimmering
tambourine, brittle with energetic music.

Sacrifice

July 1991

I hang by my obscured left foot,
my body swinging and swaying,
I feel pain as I see trees swaying-
in the cool, soft summer breeze.

There is a loose pull on my ankle
but I truly cannot see much else.
I would like to see my hanging foot,
so I imagine my foot is a hued red.

A rough crepe bandage that is
wrapped tightly around my head,
holds my two bulging eyeballs
in their sockets, prevents me so.

My foot instantly feels swollen,
it begins to emit a strong, deep
continuous throb, it throbs again,
I think I can hear drips of blood.

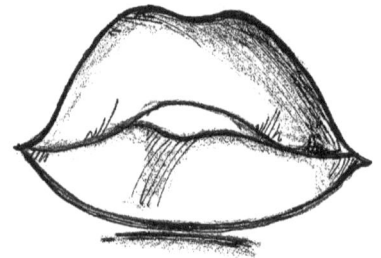

College Life

August 1991

When things go quite wrong
as sometimes they just will,
when the long road you walk
seems way up that vast hill.

When each of your assignments
are all piled way too sky-high,
when you want to laugh,
but can only let out a cry.

When you wish you hadn't woken
and you didn't want to go to class
instead, you wanted to tell all your
teachers to leave and let you pass.

When things are mixing you up,
and your life seems to be the pits,
come on over and talk with me,
because I truly love you to bits.

Plea

November 1991

Two centuries of callousness
between countless cries for help.
People killed, they had no say,
one by one, cultures vanished
the last one was a terrible day.

I know it surely was no mistake
they did no such harm to anyone,
committed not a single callous sin.
Why kill for the purpose of one's
sole appearance and toned skin?

I see the hatred in your dark eyes
imagining the dismembered forms
and each of their shattered skulls.
I hear a rifle's painful, loud signal,
please no more cruel slaying culls.

The Door

November 1991

He lay there silent
gazing at blurred images,
as tears glistened
in his saddened eye.

Sickly coloured skin
once smooth,
a mass of dark curls
now tufts of white fluff.

A sun-stroked forehead
blotched with loose flesh.
What was once pale flesh
now turned to bleached bone.

Thoughts of a deprived youth
of forgotten childhood dreams.
Scarred from frequent distress and
painful changes, he silently screams.

Nothing to feel or say
the old man dies, leaving behind
a forgotten youth, his will to live
a final desire to die.

Innocence

December 1991

In silence, he stands watching,
waiting for what is about to occur.
The first drop of gleaming liquid
hits the scuffed, grey pavement.

Relief overcomes him
thinking of only the present
not of the distant heavy future,
the drops turn into a steady flow.

He is but the innocence of life,
trapped by an overriding force
guided into darkness, he blindly
falls into the depths of a deluge.

The water rises
soon it is too deep.
His last moments
are suspended in time.

Sinking, unable to swim
he drowns. He is motionless.
Unable to alter life's time
losing control of his destiny.

The War Game

February 1992

We performed the war game
a very emotional game.
Standing in the front row
I thought they were acting.
I started to see the tears
I still kept on playing.
The shooting, the gas
the bombs soon dropped.
I had killed my friends
they were all dead.
Only now did I feel the guilt
I had been so selfish, so cruel.
It is too late now, so late
to tell them I loved them,
to give each one a helping hand.

Ponder of Love

February 1992

Love is the lingering hunger
that awaits whole satisfaction.
To manipulate, squeeze dry
and then to rapidly discard.

Some say lust, then passion
the overrated one-night stands.
Romance to flattery,
how long is it to last?

I say to listen, care
and feel to confide.
The warmth and trust
the sensitivity and respect.

You say beware, no way
stand away, don't come near.
The confusion and despair
no more time to give.

Others say chance
to grow and understand.
To turn and affront perhaps
forgiveness, possibly friends.

The Mosquito

February 1992

A mosquito flew in my window
with eyes as dark as could be.
It sprinted and flew around
it flickered and fluttered about.

I lifted my hand up so as to strike
but all it did was twiddle its thumbs.
I pretended to hurl my hand up
to make the mozzie drift away.

I thought I'd squash it on the wall
but it just glared right back at me.
The mozzie fussed its body about
as it came out of the dimmed light.

It landed on the white windowsill
I quickly squatted, squashed and
smeared the nasty little creature
with one bang from my hairbrush.

The mozzie did put up a good fight
but in the end, it did quite easily
lose to bigger me, the flat mozzie
now paralysed on my windowsill.

Exclusive

April 1992

I had loved you instead of
just anyone loving you
as a way of loving no other.
Every separate grain of your body
building the god as I built you
within me, a sealed world.
From your lips, I perhaps
learned the love of other lips.
From your starred gummed lashes
the love of other lashes.
Your shut quivering eyes
a love of other gleaming eyes.
From your body, the body
of bodies and of other bodies
in your life to greater lives.
Today, I see it is there
to be learned from you
to love what I do not own.

Love Sphere

April 1992

In our crimson love sphere
a mystical light distinguishes
us from our safe surroundings.

Amongst our friends
nothing can detract
from our united souls.

Here we are linked together
braiding life, love and passion
forming our unique existence.

Upon your gentle touch
each sensation fingers
for both of us do grow.

Against the twinkling darkness
we are seen through rose silk
it surrounds us, having no purpose.

Now, we shed our soft coating
and stand together, alone again
in our solitude, we are now one.

Handsome

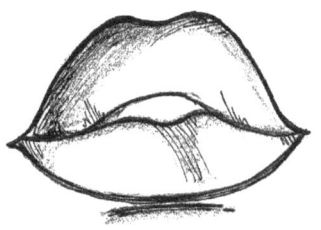

May 1992

No one but you could be any sweeter
never a doubt that you'd be a cheater.
A truly handsome yet real funny guy
so very unique and maybe a little shy.

A great person, yes, that's what I said
even unforgettable in my warm bed!
What delectable legs and that bum
even so delicious to more than some.

You showed me a sexy, sweet smile
any girl would have run a fast mile.
I'm just glad you chose zany, tiny me
because I care for you, can't you see?

Meeting your caring and sincere family
has warmed my broken heart so happily.
Even in my curiously busy frame of mind
handsome you are, so thoughtful and kind.

I really needed to see you, I did complain
I know I would have gone utterly insane.
Dirty thoughts of too much fornication
you are but my one and only medication.

The Wombat's Dilemma

August 1992

I saw a large, lazy wombat
munching on a grass root,
held way deep in his burrow-
like some secretly stolen loot.

Restless and aimlessly walking
up and down the enclosure,
I felt sorry for this little fellow
to be quite absolutely sure.

I thought how this scruffy fellow
could be out about and free,
instead of being stuck there
staring right up at strange me.

Face of Innocence

September 1992

Through my dreams,
the tears that sleep
and those that cascade
into timeless streams.

From her vivid hazel eyes
to her crimson soft lips,
to her sweet curved face
as she so sleepily lies.

The hidden soft lines
on her shadowed form,
melting intimately into
the folded sheet outlines.

Oh, dance your shadows
upon the face of innocence,
that she might also dream
in my own salty-sweet tears.

Gateway

November 1992

My heart calls with all of its voices
to hear every cell of your body sing.
The tree, through the stiffened earth
forces its strong root as it taps, taps
at the secret pleasurable love spring.

The sweet juices, without intermission
climb to the height of its olive tenement.
The breasts have borne the tender grace,
the lips have felt the pressure of content
of their own possession, with such passion.

Here I am home, within these strong arms
knowing my name, you speak with delight.
You are the dream and my gate of entry
the means by which we quietly together
slumber to waken unto the morning light.

www.ingramcontent.com/pod-product-compliance
Lightning Source LLC
Chambersburg PA
CBHW041503010526
44107CB00049B/1632